MW01248806

Fi Flap wings, fly!
love,
Jane

To all of the beautiful,
big-hearted folks
who have landed on my couch
in search of compassion
and self-acceptance.

May you wiggle your tails
forevermore.

Copyright © 2015 Jane Gross

All rights reserved. No part of this publication may be reproduced or stored in a retrieval system or transmitted in any form or by mechanical, electronic, mechanical, photocopying, recording means or otherwise without permission in writing from author/illustrator.

Library of Congress Control Number: 2015902871
CreateSpace Independent Publishing Platform, North Charleston, SC

Wiggle Your Tail

Nurturing Verse for Little Ones and Their Grown-ups

written and illustrated by Jane Gross

Trust in your Beauty

Wiggle your tail
and hold your head high.
There is only one you
from the sea
to the sky.

Your parts are all perfect
so stand up and shout,
I LOVE WHO I AM,
BOTH INSIDE AND OUT!

You Are Magic

A little, tiny tot arrived
and guess what, it was you!
And that little, tiny tot
she knew exactly what to do.

Her hands were there for grasping
and her mouth could open wide.
Her eyes were there for searching
to find love right by her side.

There is no greater magic
than that little, tiny you.
So believe me when I say this,
you've got magic here to do!

Think Happy Thoughts

When you feel a bit crabby,
alone or just blue,
remember this trick
you can do 'cause you're you!

Make believe that you're doing
the thing you love best.
Close your eyes, flap your arms
and puff out your chest.

Say OINK like a pig
who thinks she can fly
and think happy thoughts
as the clouds pass on by.

Be Amazed

Buzzing, buzzing, fuzzy bee.
Striped for all the bugs to see.
Did you fall and skin your knee?
Or did you bump into a tree?

Just when you were feeling slow
a wheel came by to help you go.

So if you're down and need a lift,
ask and you'll receive a gift.
Then like the fuzzy, buzzing bee,
you'll be amazed at what you see!

Color the World with Your Song

Sing out, sing a song,
sing with all of your heart.
Use your very own voice
and the music will start.
Take a breath, let it out,
that's the best way to go.

Your voice is a gift
that we all want to know.
Play it HIGH, play it LOW
play it LOUD, play it TRUE.

Your voice is your voice,
there's no other like you!

Imagine Flying and You Will

Dreaming is fun and easy to do!
Nothing and no one
can take it from you.

Dream of yourself
doing just what you like:
Hopping or skipping
or riding a bike.

Believe in your dreams
and know from the start,
they can really come true
when you follow your heart.

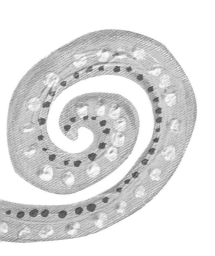

Ride the Waves

Let go
with your toes
and your hands
and your nose!

When you breathe
through the ride
your steadiness grows.

The stars in the sky
will shine down from above
and the light in your heart will
glow brighter with love.

Make A Wish

When you find a ladybug
crawling on your shirt,
pick her up with gentleness,
be careful not to hurt!

The ladybug is special
with her polka dots and all.
She offers you a wish to make,
one either large or small.

So if you find a ladybug
just sitting on your hand,
be sure to thank her very much
for knowing where to land!

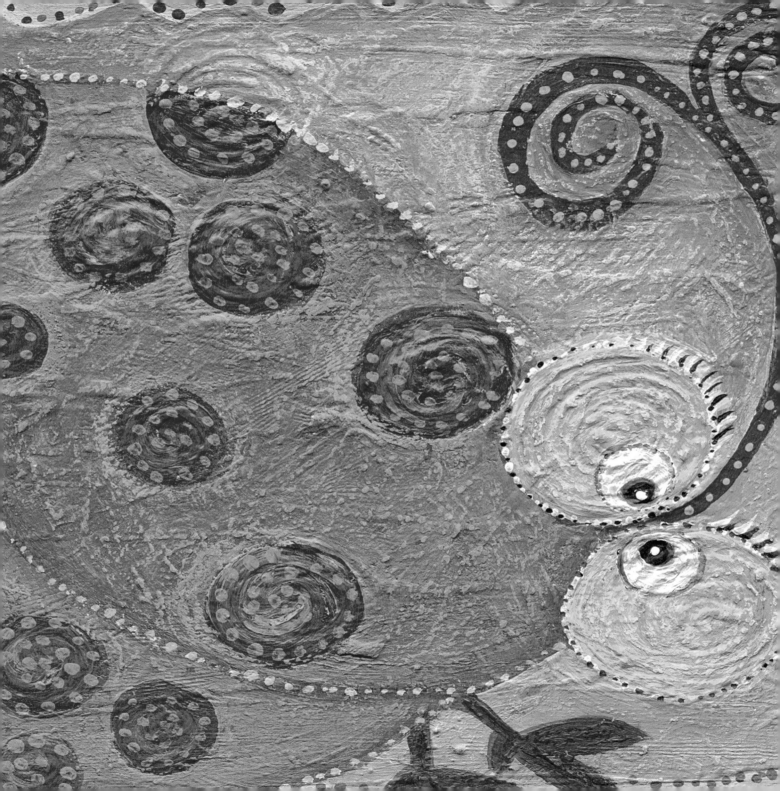

Wow! Let's Fly

Grab my hand.
Let's fly away
to places here and there.
When I have you by my side
I haven't got a care.

Dear little one,
I love you so;
let's flap our wings with glee.
Together we shall fly around
for all the world
to see.

I Love You Too!

You are my precious little one.
With you my heart does soar.
I love the way you
laugh and play.
I couldn't ask for more.

Knowing that I love you so
brings joy to every day.
And knowing that you
love me too
melts all my cares away.

Jane Gross is an artist, art therapist and
clinical social worker. She lives and works
in Connecticut, where she is currently
hatching a new series of creatures
and looking forward to hearing their
words of inspiration.

Visit her at
paintingfromtheheart.org
and
facebook.com

20229970R00015

Made in the USA
Middletown, DE
19 May 2015